FUN PARTIES FOR FUN KIDS

By Robin Graham

Illustrated by Martha Richler

Fitzhenry & Whiteside

To Jesse And Coco,

Parties were never this much fun...
until you came along.

National Library of Canada Cataloguing in Publication Data

Graham, Robin (Robin Cecile)

Fun parties for fun kids

ISBN 1-55041-610-3

1. Children's parties. I. Title.

GV1205.G72 2001   *793.2'1*   *C2001-930706-3*

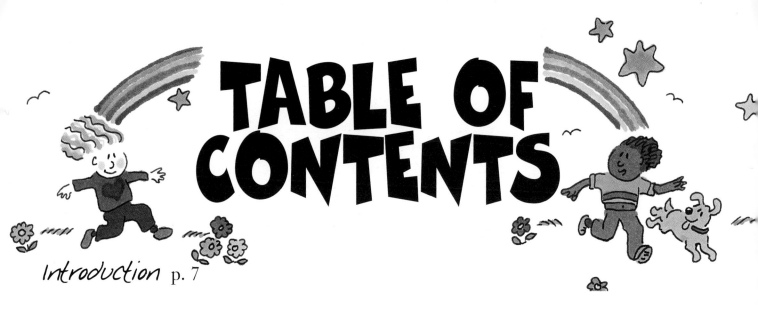

TABLE OF CONTENTS

Section C: Parties for Children Ages 7 – 10

Fun Parties For Fun Kids

INTRODUCTION

So it's birthday time again

Your kids have been reminding you for the last six months that it's *almost* their birthday. They've made a guest list that includes the whole class and half the neighbourhood, and provided you with a list of about twenty possible presents. You've heard about all the great parties they've been to, and all the loot they've brought home. Your children are pumped and excited because their special day is almost here, and they want to share it with all their friends.

Don't panic

If you have visions of ten or more children running amok in your lovely home, stopping only occasionally to shriek "What are we going to do next?" or "What kind of cake is it?" or "Where's the cat gone?" this book is perfect for you.

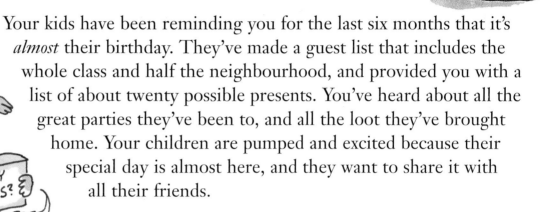

Behold in your possession, eighteen great themes for memorable parties that will be the talk of the playground. Each chapter offers a single theme with ideas for related activities, loot bag items, decorations and party favours to which you can add your own ideas.

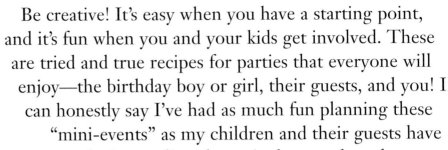

Be creative! It's easy when you have a starting point, and it's fun when you and your kids get involved. These are tried and true recipes for parties that everyone will enjoy—the birthday boy or girl, their guests, and you! I can honestly say I've had as much fun planning these "mini-events" as my children and their guests have had attending them. And remember, these guests are neither royalty nor heads of state—they're simply children who rarely register a glitch as such, and if they do, it's usually with a sense of humour.

FUN PARTIES FOR FUN KIDS also includes a chapter on Getting Started to provide you with a myriad of helpful hints that will ensure your party runs smoothly, and a section on manageable games that children love to play.

Anybody can throw a party, but not everybody throws *great* parties. Until now.

You already have the blueprints in your hands for a party your kids will always remember. All you need to add is a little time, planning and organizing.

So sit back, relax, have fun, and get ready to feel good. Believe me, it's all worth it in the end.

Fun Parties For Fun Kids

Fun Parties For Fun Kids

Fun Parties For Fun Kids

Chapter 1

YES, YOU CAN!

BOOK NOTES:

Before we jump into party basics, there are a few things you should know about this book. The following items occur with some frequency throughout, so you should understand them before proceeding.

SCHEDULES

Each chapter offers a suggested schedule, but this of course will vary, depending on the number of children you invite, the number of helping hands you've managed to coax out on party day, and the number of games and activities you choose to play or do.

A schedule is a good idea to help keep the party on track, but be *flexible*! If the children are having a good time playing the same game over and over again, or playing in the park, there's no need to jump into a new activity just because the schedule says so.

On the other hand, you don't want to have parents arriving

before the end of lunch, when there's still cake to eat and gifts to open!

You'll notice in all the schedules that opening gifts is always listed last. This is a personal preference that you may want to change, but I always like everything to be winding down by the time the gifts are brought out. If you allow gifts to be opened too early, your activities and plans will be competing with some very tempting, brand spanking new toys and games. You risk losing the birthday guests… and your own child… to the lure of the loot, and frankly, who can blame them!

Since all kids want their gifts opened first, draw names from a hat, or spin a bottle to determine the order. Avoid removing the cellophane and packaging from the gifts while everyone is still there, particularly those gifts that contain small pieces. The birthday child will be disappointed when s/he goes to play a new game for the first time, only to find a crucial piece missing that had been carelessly scattered during the party.

BE CREATIVE

You'll see a blue "Be Creative" paw print throughout this book—your chance to shine! Put on your thinking cap, let the ideas flow and then bounce them off a friend or the birthday child. You'll be amazed at how many ideas you come up with yourself that support the party's theme while adding that personal touch. Each and every time I have suggested a theme for someone who sought my advice on a home party, they have come back to tell me

Fun Parties For Fun Kids

three things: first, what a *fantastic* party they had; second, how much they *all* enjoyed it; and third (inevitably), how they *improved* it!

Every chapter is filled with great ideas, but you can make them better by tweaking them to suit you and your child, and by throwing in a couple of your own ideas.

Party photos are priceless memories that your child will enjoy looking at for years. I'm a great believer in capturing special moments on film, and I know that partygoers love to take home a memento as well.

PHOTO OP

Each party idea comes with a gold Photo Op stamp that identifies the moment for a perfect photo opportunity.

Consider these ideas:

Borrow or invest in a camera that develops photos instantly and build a craft around the photo. For example, the Beach Bash chapter gives specific instructions on a simple frame decorated with shells to house the photo, and guests can take them home as part of their loot. Frames can be created with wooden sticks, cardboard or Bristol board, and decorated to match the party's theme. Add a magnet on the back. (I usually save the advertising freebies that appear in my mailbox from pizza shops, dentists and other local businesses.) Kids will be thrilled to slap them on the fridge when they get home.

The cost of film for instant cameras can be quite pricey, but you can get around that if you live close to a 1-hour photo developer. Make sure you arrange your Photo Op early in the party and send a helper out to drop off and pick up the film. Call ahead of time or drop in the day before to explain what you want to do—they may even offer to develop the film while you wait.

If you can't develop the film immediately, glue the photo onto a folded piece of construction paper and get your child to write a simple thank-you card and sign her name. You can give them out at school the next week, drop them into guests' mailboxes or send them in the mail.

RAIN OR SHINE

These purple stamps are on chapters where the party is planned specifically for outdoors… rain or shine! Most kids need more than a little rain or snow to dampen their excitement at party time.

HEADS UP

Don't be alarmed – this ominous red stamp's bark is definitely worse than its bite! Chapters that feature this stamp are simply calling your attention to the fact that either some technical expertise may be required, a special guest needs to be invited, the activities are best suited to older children, or the party may run longer because of the complexity of the theme.

ORGANIZATION 101

A well-orchestrated party will run smoothly if you're organized, and have carefully planned as much in advance as you can. Be flexible about the results, though. Accept with grace the parts that don't work out as well as you had hoped—the fact that you ran out of time for all the games, or forgot to serve a particular food you had slaved over most of the night before, for example.

PLAN AHEAD

If you have a theme in mind, pick up items (especially dollar store trinkets) when you see them, even if the party is a month or two down the road. A beach party smack dab in the middle of winter is a ton of fun, but if you live in a colder climate, you may be hard pressed to come up with plastic pails and shovels, and other beach accessories in February. Planning way ahead in this instance would mean picking up these items on clearance in late August, and putting them away until the party. Guesstimate generously how many of everything you will need, and limit the party size accordingly when sending out invitations. If

your child's birthday falls on or around a holiday, visit stores early to get the best selection for themed items.

If you're baking a cake or cupcakes or making your own pizza crusts, do it the weekend before and put the items in the freezer. The last thing you want to be doing at 1 a.m. the night before your child's big event, is baking three dozen cupcakes with only one muffin tin.

RECRUITS

Enlisting efficient and friendly help is probably one of the most important factors for ensuring your party's success. Invite a parent or two to stay, ask a friend who knows your children well, an aunt or uncle, an older cousin, or pay your teenage neighbour a few bucks for a couple of hour's work—believe me, it's money well spent. Convince your recruits ahead of time that they'd look great in costume and delegate tasks you know they'll do well. Don't be afraid to leave them in charge while you slip away to start the food or bring out the loot bags, or assign a specific activity they can run from start to finish.

BEG, BORROW OR STEAL (well, not really)

Start calling around well in advance to borrow items you will need for the party. My phone calls always start like this: "Do you have OR do you know anyone who might have…?" You can broaden your borrowing base by asking parents who are calling to RSVP

Fun Parties For Fun Kids

the party—they will always oblige since their own children are guests, and they can usually retrieve the borrowed item when they come to pick up their kids. Be diligent about returning items you borrow when you say you will, and don't borrow anything you're not prepared to replace if necessary.

TIPS ON WORKING WITH KIDS

Not all children are alike. For every ten sweet, well-mannered children that are in attendance, there will be one who doesn't listen, doesn't participate, yells out the answers to all the questions you ask before anyone else, wants to open the gifts immediately, and generally spends the entire party teetering on your very last nerve… or your husband's.

Patience

You will need lots of it, especially if you're bravely entertaining a large group. Having helpers at the party will dilute a troublesome child's effect on you, and you can take turns keeping him or her in check.

Flexibility

There will be lots of personalities to consider, and you will probably have to do some good-natured, last minute juggling to accommodate the guests. For example, although most kids LOVE to put on shows, especially if their parents are in the audience, a shy guest may prefer to open and close the curtains, start the music or operate the lights. At game time, some children may opt out for whatever reasons—in a team situation, be prepared to sub in a fun dad or an older cousin who happens to be on hand.

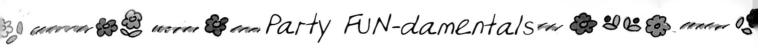

Grouping Children

You will notice our birthday groups are often broken down into smaller, more manageable groups upon arrival. By assigning an adult helper to each group, the children are receiving more of the individual one-on-one attention they all enjoy. In addition, children won't get bored or restless waiting for their turn and, if only five are painting at any one time, you won't need to buy enough paint pots and brushes for twenty kids.

Selecting a Party theme

Take your time selecting the theme for your child's birthday, with their help, of course. All good marketers understand how important it is to KNOW YOUR AUDIENCE, and the same can be said for party planning. Some themes just naturally lend themselves toward one sex over another, particularly in the parties aimed at older children. While you would no more expect a rowdy group of children with a collective case of ants in their pants to lay out a newspaper and write the stories for it, you would hardly encourage a quiet, crafty bunch to run the tires on an obstacle course at the football training camp… rain or shine!

INVITATIONS

Making your own invitations is the first opportunity you have to sit down with the birthday boy or girl, and together, launch the theme. Use construction paper and stick-ers, cut pictures from mag-azines, print graphics from your computer to glue on or, print the whole

* SCRAPS OF OLD FABRIC

* SCISSORS * GLUE * CONSTRUCTION PAPER

GLUE

* WOOL

18

Fun Parties For Fun Kids

personalized invitation using a simple computer program with graphics.

Ensure special instructions are clearly communicated, especially if the party will be held outdoors, rain or shine. Similarly, if you're inviting twelve 6-year-olds to

Chef-for-a-day, make sure they come dressed appropriately. Removing pizza sauce from a pair of denim overalls is a lot easier than trying to get the same off a velvet party dress.

Also, be very clear if you want children to bring anything with them, such as a stuffed friend for the Teddy Bear's Picnic. It never hurts to remind parents when they call to RSVP of your special plans for the day.

A WORD (or two) ABOUT DOLLAR STORES / PARTY STORES

I just don't know what we did before the advent of dollar stores, but now that they're here to stay, get to know your local outlets… intimately! When planning a party, visit early and often as stock changes constantly and is often of the mystery variety.

Buy craft supplies, prizes, inexpensive decorations such as streamers, balloons and Bristol board, paper products and loot bag filler. Look for interesting containers to

serve as the loot "bags," such as plastic vanities, plastic pencil cases, baskets, plastic pumpkins, pails, makeup cases or small bags with handles.

Take a list of specific items you're looking for but do take a few extra minutes to walk every single aisle in the store. Look for items that are new since your last visit, and be open to add and substitute list items when you find something better… and you will!

LOOT BAGS

If you've ever felt that despite the incredible party you threw, you were ultimately judged on your loot bag-ability, you're not alone. One could single-handedly lead twenty three 8-year-olds up the rock face of Everest on a hiking trip, and the result would still be the same. At my children's last Halloween party (with no birthday attached), after two and a half hours of non-stop fun, games and food, partygoers were both stunned and incredulous that there were no loot bags.

Like it or not, loot bags are a fact of life—just accept it and go with it.

Consider the following ideas when planning the loot:

Buy one great item in keeping with the theme and add loot bag filler—candy, chocolate, gum, potato chips, pencils, stickers (available in practically every theme imaginable!), colouring books, markers and/or hair accessories, for example.

Use plain brown or white lunch sacs for the loot bags and write the children's names on the bags with bright and colourful markers. Decorate with stickers.

Alternatively, give children an empty paper sac with their name on it, and let them "shop" for their own loot. Have

Fun Parties For Fun Kids

bowls or baskets filled with various items and let them pick one thing from each.

If you feel like splurging or loot bags really aren't your thing, party stores often have attractive, pre-made loot bags in a variety of price ranges.

Prizes

Games are always fun when they end in prizes, but don't lose any sleep over what to give out.

Homemade "Winner" ribbons and medals are just fine—so are pieces of bubble gum, lollipops or small bags of chips.

Prizes shouldn't be so grand that children are mortally disappointed when they don't win, and everyone should get a prize of some sort at the conclusion of the games.

A fun idea is to give out tokens or pennies as prizes that can be kept in small, labelled paper cups, and then cashed in at the end of the games at the "prize table" (dollar store items, candy and gum grandly displayed as prizes on a "special" table covered with a cloth).

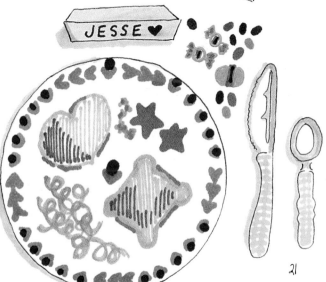

Food

Concentrate on kid-friendly foods that can be dressed up for the party: bake curly fries instead of plain, cut carrots and celery with a wavy blade and serve with dip. Use large cookie cutters to cut grilled cheese sandwiches in a variety of shapes (these can be cut the night before, and stored on baking pans between sheets of wax paper).

Use colourful party ware at the table, and decorate the table with theme items.

If you've accumulated a huge basketful of those plastic toys from fast food restaurants over the years, use them to decorate platters of sandwiches or on top of the cake, as centrepieces, or at each child's place.

PARENTS AND HELPERS

Finally, you're ready for the party and everything's coordinated—from the activities to the decorations to the loot bags to the birthday child. After all this planning, are you really going to open the front door in your jeans and T-shirt?

Of course not!

Moms, Dads and helpers, don't forget your craziest Hawaiian print shirt, your eye patch and striped jersey, your teddy bear hairband and blackened nose, your multicoloured clown wig, your old bridesmaid dress and whatever else you can come up with!

GAMES GALORE

A few well-organized games will go a long way toward burning off excess energy, filling time… and, of course, entertaining the guests.

Here are some ideas for easy games that children love to play. Remember, kids love when adults participate as well, so throw in your helpers and a dad or two.

For the Younger Crowd:
Pin the Tail on the Donkey

A classic party game available at both dollar and party stores, sometimes with variations like Pin the Nose on the Clown. You can easily make your own theme game for the party like Pin the Tail on the Bunny for the Magic Party, Pin the Eye Patch on the Pirate at the Scavenger Hunt, or Pin the Sail on the Boat at the Beach Party.

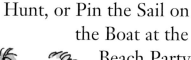
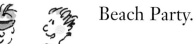

Games Galore

Musical Chairs

Little ones love the thrill of this old favourite, and the rules are easy for any age to understand.

A fun, older-child variation is to have the children sit in a circle and line up stuffed animals in the middle. Like musical chairs, there should be the same number of animals as children LESS ONE, and when the music stops, they all try to snatch an animal. Whoever doesn't get one is out, and the game continues until there is a winner.

If you ever noticed that musical chairs can get a little boisterous, this version can be even more rambunctious with the older kids.

Substitute items that are in theme with the party for the stuffed animals if you wish.

Duck, Duck, Goose

Another kid favourite and, with no props required, a mom-and-dad favourite as well!

Seat the children in a circle, and have the birthday child start the game by walking around the outside of the circle, patting his friends on the head while saying, "Duck…duck…duck…" with each pat. The fun starts when he pats someone and says "Goose," then starts to run around the circle. The child whose head has been "Goose-patted" jumps up and runs in the opposite direction, each with the goal of reaching the vacated spot first and sitting down in it. Whoever doesn't get the spot starts patting heads again.

This game has no real end, but you can stop after each child has had a turn running the circle at least once.

For a variation, use theme words like Teddy, Teddy, BEAR, Beach, Beach, BALL, or Pepperoni, Pepperoni, PIZZA!

Games Galore

Statue

Get the kids dancing to their favourite pop songs and stop the music at various intervals. The object is to stand as still as a "statue" once the music stops and to start dancing again only after the music is turned back on. Kids that are caught moving are eliminated from the game, and play continues until there is one person left. Don't be afraid to call a tie if the last two or three are close.

Hot Potato

With kids sitting in a circle, tossing the "hot potato" one by one around the circle, turn music off and on as above. Whoever is caught with the "hot potato" when the music stops is out, and play continues until there is one person left.

"Hot potatoes" can be anything from balls to bean bags to stuffed animals. Even a glob of joke store slime is a fun choice, guaranteed to have the kids shrieking with delight each time they touch it!

Limbo

With two people, each holding one end of a broom or mop handle, have kids limbo their way, one at a time, under the pole. Lower the pole after everyone has had a turn at the first height, and continue in this manner to see who can go the lowest.

Games Galore

What's missing?

Place 8-12 items on a tray and let everyone study them for two minutes. At the end of the study time, take the tray out of sight and remove one item. See who can identify which item has been removed first. Repeat, removing different items each time.

You can vary the number of items on the tray, depending on the age of your guests, and vary the selection of items, depending on your theme.

FOR THE OLDER KIDS:

Dangling Donuts

Cut even lengths of kitchen string, tie mini donuts to one end, and tie stringed donuts, two or three at a time onto a broom or mop handle. Divide children into two or three teams, and have one player from each team start.

With their hands behind their backs, the children race against each other to eat their entire donut that is dangling in front of their faces from the pole, held up on either side by two adults.

Swing the donuts gently to make it more difficult, and use the powdered-sugar variety for some messy fun!

Note: this game can take a long time if it's a large party!

Bingo

Buy an inexpensive Bingo set and get busy calling numbers—kids LOVE to play Bingo!

Use pattern variations in addition to full-card Bingo to keep the game moving along quickly and to provide more exciting prize opportunities.

If you're feeling particularly ambitious, make your own Bingo cards, using icons in the party theme and pennies as markers.

Games Galore

Future Stars

See Chapter 20, "Superstar," for instructions.

FOR ALL AGES:

Relay Races

Relay races are lots of fun at a party because kids get to work together as teams.

Try variations like running back and forth with an egg on a teaspoon, 3-legged style where two children have one leg each tied together, or wheelbarrow, where, again working in pairs, one child holds the other's legs up and that child walks on his hands.

A particular favourite among children is the Bigfoot relay, where each team starts with a pile of adult clothing, a pair of big shoes (try Dad's) and some accessories like a hat, sunglasses, and a watch, for example. The first group of children has to put on all the clothes, accessories and shoes, and clomp as fast as they can to their partner team. Each child then strips off all the Bigfoot clothing and shoes, and the next child in line puts it on, and so on.

Games Galore

Skills Competitions

Skills competitions also make good party games and they don't have to be complicated. If you have a basketball hoop on your driveway, line the party guests up for free throws. Have a putting contest inside or out, a ring toss or dart contest. You can even give each child a piece of paper to make a paper airplane, and see whose plane flies the furthest.

Fun Parties For Fun Kids

Chapter 3
LET'S HAVE A PARADE!

PLAN YOUR SCHEDULE

Parade Prep	30 minutes
Actual parade (and photos)	30 minutes
Games	15 minutes
Lunch and Cake	30 minutes
Gifts	15 minutes
TOTAL	**2 HOURS**

What child doesn't love a parade?
Here's a chance to actually be in one!

This idea works well with a large group of kids, because there are so many roles involved in staging a parade.

GETTING READY

Get all your props together

LOOT BAGS Add kazoos or other noise-makers, balloons, flags, foam clown noses, face paint and/or temporary tattoos.

Think of the parades you've been to, and all the different people in the procession. Have a parade-master with a megaphone at the front, announcing "Jesse's Birthday Parade" to the neighbourhood. Perhaps some of the parents (or even friendly neighbours who have been advised in advance) may have time to come out to the parade route and honk horns or cheer on the children. Have two kids carry the banner, waving to the "crowds." Feature a clown with some balloons and a pom-pom girl or boy. Instruments—a drum and cymbals (get creative and substitute pots and pans and wooden spoons if you like), and a trumpet or kazoo, for example—will attract attention. Giftwrap a large box or two, leaving the bottom open, and cut a hole in the top for the kids' heads to poke through. Stick a bow on top of their heads, and you've got a couple of walking-talking presents in your parade.

Floats are easy to make with a couple of wagons festooned with crepe streamers, and filled with stuffed animals. One wagon could carry a boom box playing a tape or CD of favourite songs the kids could sing along with while they're marching. Get (or make) a cape and a crown for the King or Queen of the Parade (the birthday boy or girl). Buy some inexpensive funny hats and flags at the dollar store, and some face paint as well. If you have a pet, bring it along and dress it up too—your dog will look adorable with an antler headband and your cat will be the best-dressed feline in a sporty bow tie.

Fun Parties For Fun Kids

Parties for Ages 4-6

Plan the parade route

It can be as simple as around the block, or it can be longer, depending on the age of the kids. Use your own child as a reference point.

Assign roles in advance

Decide before the party who should be what and write it down. If you wait until the party to ask who wants to be a clown, you may find yourself in the unfortunate position of having to pick between six 5-year-olds—all with their hands up.

Enlist help

Depending on the number of children, you may wish to have a few other adults to help—at least to march alongside to ensure you return with the same number of children you had when you started. Extra help would also be appreciated when you're preparing for the parade, handing out the props and painting the children's faces.

Start the banner

Using a roll of paper, cut a banner approximately 6 feet long by 2 $\frac{1}{2}$ feet wide. Write the name of your child's parade in large letters, and mount on two broom or mop handles. Alternatively, you may wish to use two smaller signs on pieces of Bristol board, each mounted on a mop or broom handle, or worn like a sandwich board.

PARTY TIME!

When all the guests have arrived, tell them what their part in the parade will be. If you have not yet decided, throw all the different roles into a hat, and let each child pick one out.

Divide the group into two smaller sets, and let one half begin decorating and personalizing

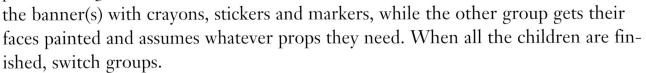

the banner(s) with crayons, stickers and markers, while the other group gets their faces painted and assumes whatever props they need. When all the children are finished, switch groups.

Line the kids up outside in the order in which they'll be marching, but don't worry if they rearrange themselves en route. Encourage the kids to wave and sing, and remember, kids like to have an example to follow!!

Follow the rest of your schedule, and enjoy the parade!

PHOTO OP
Have each party guest stand under the banner with the birthday boy or girl, or take a shot of the whole group standing under the banner, which can be copied for each guest.

C h a p t e r   4

DINO DIG

Digging for fossils is just part of this exciting adventure party!

PLAN YOUR SCHEDULE

Dino Dig prep	15 minutes
Hike to fossil site	15 minutes
Dino Dig	30 minutes
Games	15 minutes
Lunch and cake	30 minutes
Gifts	15 minutes
TOTAL	2 HOURS

FOSSIL SITE

Parties for Ages 4-6

GETTING READY

Decide on the location of the dig

Pick a quiet public playground with a sandbox that could be commandeered by your gang of archaeologists-in-training. If you want to do it in your backyard, you can purchase a few bags of sand inexpensively, and dump them in an old plastic swimming pool that can double as the "fossil site" for the party.

IMPORTANT If you decide to use a public sandbox, be prepared to turn the sand and rake it thoroughly before your party to ensure there is nothing dangerous hidden below the surface.

check out the store at a natural history museum!

Shop for your fossil treasures

Visit your dollar store and stock up on goodies the kids can dig for.

Be Creative

Look for plastic vampire fangs (Tyrannosaurus teeth), plastic dog bones (Triceratops bones), plastic eggs (belonging to a Velociraptor, of course), fake claws and skulls. If you feel particularly energetic, create your own "fossils" by pressing a variety of small rubber reptiles, snails and shells into molding clay, and leave them to harden until the day of the party.

LOOT BAGS Add dinosaur books, stickers and candies, shark tooth necklaces, "camp" hats and animal-shaped crackers to the pails as the kids are leaving.

MODELLING CLAY
WASHABLE

measuring jug ↓
WATER

disposable plastic or foil dish ↓

shells

4 BILLION YRS OLD
↑
molding clay

(collection of wierd rubber reptiles)

Fun Parties For Fun Kids

Parties for Ages 4-6

← expedition hat

J.R. J.R.

← penknife

Binoculars ✓
magnifying
glass ✓
bone ✓
toothbrush ✓
notebook ✓

Shop for your props too

While shopping for your treasures, start assembling the props that will end up as part of the party loot. Buy plastic pails, shovels, picks and sieves, toy magnifying glasses, field notebooks and colourful dinosaur pencils. Label each pail with a guest's name in advance, and pack everything else inside.

Make a discovery chart

Using a large piece of paper, sketch the "fossils" the kids will be digging for, and label each one. If you prefer, you can take photos of the fossils, and stick them on the discovery chart instead.

School

N
W — E
S

BIRCH AVE

my house

PARKING LOT

PARK

FOSSIL SITE Swings

CIRCLE RD

* sandbox

Make a map leading to the fossil site

Buy a piece of parchment from a craft store and draw a map of your neighbourhood, ending at the fossil site at the park, or back at your yard. Use trees, houses and fences as landmarks along the way. Plan to plant a few arrowheads, skulls and a pile of rocks on the route the day of the party, and include these on your map. If you have a bright and sunny day, use sidewalk chalk for additional clues and directions.

JESSE   COCO

PARTY TIME!

When all the guests have assembled, have the birthday boy or girl hand out the pails. Ask the children to decorate and write their names or initials on all the contents, so at the end of the party, they will be able to distinguish their own tools from those of their friends.

Unroll the "ancient" parchment map with great flourish, and explain the "mission" to the children. As the expedition leader, be sure to bring a pair of binoculars and a pocketknife with you on the hike. Don't forget to dress the part, with a floppy camp hat, fishing vest and hiking boots. Pause often to let each child look through the binoculars, and use every gadget on your knife in some official way to show you've done this many times before.

When you arrive at the fossil site, show the junior paleontologists the discovery chart, so they have an idea of what they're digging for. Throw all the kids' names in a hat and pull out one at a time, indicating the order in which they will dig. If you let all the kids dig at once, it's possible some children might end up empty-handed—and very disappointed.

PHOTO OP
Be sure to gather the kids around the birthday child at the fossil site, and have them raise their shovels and yell "Dino Dig!" on the count of 3.

Depending on the size of your fossil site, you may wish to hide a few fossils before the diggers arrive, and then add a few more at intervals between digging. Have an adult helper distract the kids with a possible dinosaur sighting (that turns out to be a dog), or show them a previously undiscovered lizard on a nearby tree. When all else fails, break out the surprise snacks while more fossils are secretly added to the site.

EXHIBIT A
VELOCIRAPTOR EGG

Demonstrate initially how to dig gently for fossils, how to sift the sand, and how to remove fossils carefully once a tool has made contact.

Encourage the children to take notes as their friends dig. They can record the weather, include a drawing of what each person found, and any other details they wish to include in their books.

As each child makes their own exciting discovery, have them identify their find on the chart, and sign their name to it. The chart will make an excellent keepsake for the birthday child, and a very interesting item for Show and Tell at a later date.

If you're at a public park, let the kids run

around for a few minutes before returning home. If you want to organize a couple of games, try the Bigfoot relay, to which you can donate your binoculars, wide-brimmed hat and cargo vest. Alternatively, you can call out a guest's name and see who can remember what his or her discovery was, OR, using the Discovery Chart, point to the pictures, and see who remembers who found each item.

Follow the rest of the schedule and enjoy the dig!

C h a p t e r 5

CHEF-FOR-A-DAY

Kids love to help out in the kitchen, so why not let them prepare all the food? This party works with as many children as your kitchen can accommodate.

PLAN YOUR SCHEDULE

Craft(s)	15 minutes
Pizza prep	15 minutes
Baking time/Games	15 minutes
Lunch	15 minutes
Cupcake decorating	15 minutes
Games	30 minutes
Cake and gifts	15 minutes
TOTAL	2 HOURS

GETTING READY

LOOT BAGS Include the cupcake, chef's hat and craft, as well as miniature baking pans, cookie cutters and/or a kids recipe book.

Decide on your menu

The easiest menu items, both in terms of preparation and kid appeal, are pizza and cupcakes. Even with the simplest of menus, you will be running back and forth, so concentrate on just a couple of foods to keep the little ones busy.

For the pizza, you can opt for a homemade crust, store-bought pizza dough, pitas or English muffins, depending on how energetic you're feeling. Buy aluminum pie plates for each child, so they have their own personal pans. You can buy a variety of toppings in addition to pizza sauce to broaden the design possibilities, but keep in mind that most young children are quite content with a plain cheese pizza or cheese and pepperoni.

le menu

bonjour mes amis!

"le pizza"

"les cupcakes"

"les cookies"

For the cupcakes, bake them in advance if you can in colourful paper baking cups, and have the children frost and decorate them. Visit your nearby bulk retailer and stock up on an assortment of sprinkles, quins (tiny, brightly coloured candy shapes often themed for approaching occasions like Christmas or Valentine's Day), gumdrops, jelly beans, mini

candy-coated chocolates, licorice and coconut—the more the merrier! Buy lots of variety in small quantities, which you can set out in small bowls, aluminum tart pans or saucers—be prepared for some furtive nibbling during the decorating fun!

Make a basic white frosting in advance, or buy it from a bakery or the supermarket, and tint it in lots of colours. If you're working on a large table or counter, set out several small groupings of various colours with plastic knives, to eliminate several children clamouring impatiently for the same colour.

Decide on a craft (or two!)

Paper chef hats are inexpensive and can be acquired from a restaurant supply store. They can be decorated with brightly coloured markers and stickers, and can be personalized across the front band with each child's name.

Inexpensive wooden spoons can be painted, personalized, decorated with dried flowers, tied with a pretty plaid ribbon bow and sent home for children to hang proudly in their own kitchens.

cheese

Enlist help

The party will run a lot smoother with a few extra pairs of hands to assist in the kitchen and with the crafts.

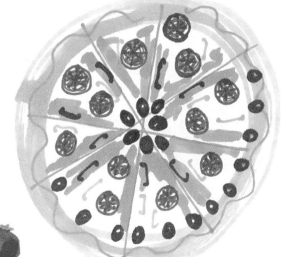

peppers

olives

sliced tomato

PARTY TIME!

Greet children wearing an apron and a chef's hat, and welcome them to the birthday boy or girl's restaurant. A Bristol board sign on the front door made in advance by you and the birthday child saying "Chez Corey" or "Brendan's Diner" will set the tone for the chef theme.

Organize the crafts immediately so the junior chefs can actually wear their hats for the food prep. If you're doing both crafts, divide into two groups and then switch upon completion.

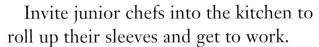

Invite junior chefs into the kitchen to roll up their sleeves and get to work.

Although enough cheese for the pizzas has been grated in advance, have a manageable block of cheese on hand that the kids can take turns grating. Make sure it's large enough to avoid grating little fingers, and have this activity well supervised by an adult.

Lead the children through each stage, spreading the sauce, laying the pepperoni slices and sprinkling the cheese, encouraging them to experiment with various designs—like funny faces, or initials, for example. Stick toothpicks with each child's name into their pizzas before baking to avoid any mix-ups at lunchtime.

While the pizzas are baking, organize a few simple games such as What's Missing, using miscellaneous kitchen gadgets and items.

Have helpers pretend to be managers, waiters and hostesses at the restaurant.

Wear a silly moustache, adopt a funny accent, anything goes!

Have simple photocopied menus with a picture party guests can colour, and crayons at each place setting to continue the restaurant theme.

After lunch, organize the cupcake decorating, giving each child two cupcakes—one to eat at cake time, and one to take home and show off to their parents as part of their loot.

Follow the rest of the schedule, and enjoy the eats!

PHOTO OP
Get a shot of each guest with the birthday boy or girl in the kitchen, in front of the oven or sitting together on the counter. Put aprons on them, give each a wooden spoon, grater or other kitchen item and smudge a little flour on each one's nose for fun.

C h a p t e r   6

SUPERHERO/ PRINCESS PARTY

*Kids come dressed as their favourite Superhero or Princess...
and meet a real live one at the party!*

PLAN YOUR SCHEDULE

Special Guest Greeting	15 minutes
Craft	30 minutes
Games	30 minutes
Lunch and Cake	30 minutes
Gifts	15 minutes
TOTAL	2 HOURS

Parties for Ages 4-6

This is a party that requires some dramatic licence on the part of your special guest.

GETTING READY

Invite a Superhero or Princess

Nothing will make the birthday child feel more special than co-hosting his or her birthday party with a Superhero or a Princess—even if it turns out to be a favourite aunt or uncle, friend or babysitter. Personality is everything, so select an adult who has LOTS of energy, LOTS of patience and relates well to children (not just yours).

Be Creative

If you feel like spending money, rent a costume for your guest. If not, a Superhero could be dark and mysterious, in a black turtleneck and black jeans, with a makeshift cape, cowboy boots, a hat, a black eye-mask, and a pencil-thin moustache. OR, he could be goofy, in bright tights with crazy boxer shorts, sneakers with mismatched socks, and an old T-shirt with some painted proclamation of his greatness (i.e. Super Ryan—Master of All).

A princess could recycle an old bridesmaid dress (the one you said you'd NEVER wear again, and

LOOT BAGS
For Superheroes, look for themed trading cards, comic books, doodle kits and/or notebooks.
For Princesses, include play makeup, nail polish, storybooks, jewellery, tiaras and/or doodle kits.

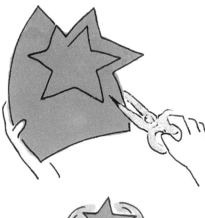

believe me, the more elaborate it is, the more impressive it will be), borrow a wig, add a crown and some dainty gloves. While little girls are generally enamoured of the Very Together Princess, a little goofy can be fun here too—try hair slightly askew, runs in her stockings, mismatched shoes, squinting at everyone and bumping into walls until she finds her huge oversized glasses.

Plan your guest's role

A Superhero could demonstrate some Karate moves, lead a spirited game of Simon Says, tell a real life adventure story, apply tattoos and help the pint-size heroes make their own Superhero masks. Buy masks at the party store, and let kids decorate them with glitter glue, stickers and markers. Alternatively, use face paint to create the Superhero look with lightning bolts, scars and other appropriate markings.

A Princess could read or tell a story, apply nail polish, do fancy hairdos and apply makeup. Have a variety of lipsticks, eye shadows and polishes for girls to choose from. She could also help the girls make their own crowns from precut Bristol board, using cotton balls, glitter, foil shapes and dollar store jewels to decorate.

Bake or order a special cake to support the theme—a variety of specialty pans are often available for rental at bulk stores, bakeries and party rental stores.

PARTY TIME!

When all the guests have arrived, assemble them into one area to prepare for the Superhero or Princess guest's grand entrance. If possible, try to make this a surprise for everyone, including the birthday child. Use appropriate music to help with the introduction and add to the excitement of the moment.

Give your special guest a list of the children in attendance, so they can call each one up individually to meet and greet them and shake their hands (much like a visiting Santa). Ask the guest to comment on something specific to each child, such as what he or she is wearing or anything special that's been added to his or her costume.

Organize the crafts, and divide into smaller groups as necessary. Make sure each group is able to spend time with the Superhero or Princess.

Have the guest sit at the table with the children, next to the birthday boy or girl.

Name your menu items to coincide with your theme—Powerman Pasta, Superkid Spaghetti, Mystical Macaroni and Crown Jewel Cake are a few examples.

Follow the rest of your schedule and enjoy the stars!

PHOTO OP
Seat the Superhero or Princess guest in a special chair, and flank them on either side with each guest and the birthday child, for individual shots.

C h a p t e r   7

TEDDY BEAR PICNIC

An opportunity to show off a favourite stuffed friend to favourite real friends!
For the younger ones, what could be more fun than a simple picnic party in the park?

PLAN YOUR SCHEDULE

Hand out baskets/ walk to park	15 minutes
Games	30 minutes
Lunch and cake	20 minutes
Playing in the park	25 minutes
Walk home/Gifts	30 minutes
TOTAL	2 HOURS

Parties for Ages 4-6

GETTING READY

LOOT BAGS
Pack small stuffed animals, plastic picnic items, colouring books and crayons and other loot bag items in a small wicker basket.

Invitations

Make two invitations—one for the guest, and one for the guest's stuffed friend!

Decide where you will have the party

Ideally, this party is best suited for outdoors, but be prepared to move inside, in case of inclement weather. If you live within walking distance of a park, plan on having the party there and returning to the house to open gifts.

Get your picnic props together

Get a few old blankets or throws to spread on the grass for the children and their animals. Borrow picnic baskets from friends, neighbours and the parents of your guests. Use backpacks or even small baskets with handles and bright checked napkins, so each guest can carry something.

Decide on the picnic food

Plan a menu of easy-to-pack items—sandwiches cut into different shapes, potato chips, Cheesies, juice

DRAW - A - BEAR KIT

① DRAW A LINE DOWN THE CENTRE OF A SHEET OF CONSTRUCTION PAPER:

4 EASY STEPS TO CREATE YOUR OWN TEDDY-BEAR INVITATION!

② NOW DRAW YOUR BEAR, MAKING SURE THE PAWS TOUCH YOUR LINE:

④ NOW DECORATE YOUR BEAR WITH MARKERS AND GLITTER!

③ FOLD YOUR SHEET OF PAPER IN TWO, AND CUT OUT YOUR TEDDY-BEAR SHAPE...

YOU'RE INVITED ♥ TO MY ♥ TEDDY BEAR PICNIC!

Don't forget your teddy bear!

date ———
time ———
address ———

tel.

P.S. YOUR BEAR CAN BE ANY COLOUR AT ALL!

boxes, carrots, celery, pickles, grapes, apples, for example. Buy colourful paper plates and bring party hats, personalized and decorated with teddy bear stickers, to wear at the park.

Get some music

Arrange to bring along a boom box with pre-made tapes of the children's favourite songs, including of course, "Teddy Bear's Picnic."

Enlist help

A few extra hands will come in handy to help carry the bulkier and heavier items, and a few extra pairs of eyes can help supervise on the playground.

PARTY TIME!

Once all the guests have arrived, hand out the baskets or backpacks. Line the partygoers up and walk to the park, singing a song or playing Follow the Leader.

Upon arrival at the park, stake out a suitable area and lay out your blankets. Ideally, another adult could have gone ahead earlier and staked out the area, using gardening poles and brightly coloured streamers or colourful mini-flag garlands. A hand-lettered sign on a wooden pole that says "Mackenzie's Teddy Bear Picnic" could be erected to welcome guests.

Settle everyone in a circle on the blankets and get each child to introduce his or her stuffed animal. Play games that involve the animals such as going around the circle, having each child name as many of the animals as they can.

Alternatively, put all the stuffed animals together on one blanket, throw all their names in a hat, and have each child draw a name and try to pick out the corresponding animal. Give bonus points to children who can return the animals to their

PHOTO OP
Seat each guest with the birthday child on the blanket with all the stuffed animals for a classic Teddy Bear Picnic shot.

rightful owners.

Organize a few simple games like Simon Says and Relay Races.

Have one blanket designated for food and drinks, one for animals, and a couple for the party guests. Bring plastic cups and saucers for the stuffed animals, and put small plates of food (real or fake) on their blanket as well.

Set ground rules for playground play after lunch. If the park is busy, assign each adult a group of four children or less, and let children know who their group leader is. If the picnic is in your backyard or inside, have a few extra games or a craft organized.

Follow the rest of your schedule and enjoy the picnic.

C h a p t e r   8

MAGIC TIME

A magic show where the kids go behind the wand
Here's a party where kids see a magic show, learn the tricks and
put on a show for their parents.

COCO'S MAGIC SHOW

PLAN YOUR SCHEDULE

Magician's show	15 minutes
Magic school	30 minutes
Lunch and cake	30 minutes
Gifts	15 minutes
Rehearsal	15 minutes
Kids show	15 minutes
TOTAL	**2 HOURS**

Parties for Ages 4-6

A special guest with some magical expertise will be required, or alternatively, some heavy-duty hands-on research.

GETTING READY

LOOT BAGS
Look for stuffed bunnies, wands, dollar store magic tricks, decks of cards and/or invisible ink pads.

Invitations

Ask parents to come back fifteen minutes earlier to pick up their children so they can watch their kids perform in the magic show.

Plan the magic show

Hire a magician if you feel like splurging, or engage an adult or older teenager to act as a magician.

If you decide to do-it-yourself, visit your local library and borrow a couple of books that show simple magic tricks and card tricks, and have your magician learn a few. Invest in an inexpensive magic set that has all the props for approximately ten tricks, and learn those too.

Remember, in a room full of six-year-olds, a little flourish and some distracting music and lighting will greatly aid the amateur sleight of hand.

Parties for Ages 4-6

Get your props together

Hang two dark sheets, decorated with foil or shiny fabric star cutouts. Set up a table with a similarly decorated tablecloth in front of the curtains.

Have all the props arranged on a table off to the side. Set up chairs or plan to have the children seated on the floor in front of where the magician will perform.

Get out the welcome mat

Make a sign for the front door that says "Welcome to Jennifer's School of Magic" and decorate it with stars and moons.

PARTY TIME!

When all the guests have arrived, welcome them to the School of Magic and introduce the Guest Magician. Make up a name like "The Great Nicoleski" or "The Mysterious Mr. Magic" and stay with it for the whole party.

After the magician finishes his show, ask children, trick by trick, who would like to perform each one for the Parents Show after lunch. In the case of many raised hands, throw names in a hat, or alternatively, let more than one child perform the same trick during the Kids Show. Parents won't mind, and everyone will be happy.

Divide the children into groups to learn the tricks at Magic School. Depending on the number of children at the party, you may need to assign Magician and Assistant roles for each trick that will be performed for the parents.

> ### PHOTO OP
> *Take individual photos with magician flanked on both sides by the birthday child and one guest at a time, with the curtain backdrop. Alternatively, take photos of each child receiving their diploma from the magician.*

Be Creative

Remember to inject some cornball fun into the performances such as flamboyant self-introductions, showmanship, drum rolls and APPLAUSE signs.

Get everyone ready after lunch by having a quick rehearsal before the parents arrive.

After the show, have the magician call children up individually and present them with preprinted "Diplomas" from Magic School in front of their parents.

Chapter 9

PIRATES SCAVENGER HUNT

Ahoy, Matey! Kids follow simple clues to find the pirate's treasure.

PLAN YOUR SCHEDULE

Assigning groups	15 minutes
Scavenger Hunt	45 minutes
Games	15 minutes
Lunch and cake	30 minutes
Gifts	15 minutes
TOTAL	**2 HOURS**

Parties for Ages 4-6

Though this party requires a bigger commitment in terms of advance planning, party day is relatively easy because of it.

GETTING READY

Decide where your Scavenger Hunt will take place

A hunt around the neighbourhood is an excellent idea, ending up either at a nearby park or in your backyard.

Decide how many groups you will have

Groups of four to five children will work best, because it gives everyone a chance to actively participate—answering questions, spotting clues and solving riddles, for example. Design a hunt for each group with 15-20 questions each.

Be Creative

Start by telling the children which way to turn at the bottom of the driveway, and which way to turn at every corner. Have them search for unusual things in the neighbourhood such as a pink garage door (the entrance to Mermaid Lagoon), a flag (of a friendly neighbouring country) or a boat in the driveway (One-Eyed Willy's pirate ship). Ask neighbours you know for permission to hang a pirate hook or stuffed parrot on a fence post, or a sign in the window. On a dry day, use sidewalk chalk to give additional instructions along the route. Set up checkpoints with a friendly pirate stamping hands, putting stickers on cheeks or handing out balloons. Have other check-

points where the children will have to get past the crusty old pirate who makes them each "walk the plank" (using a low-to-the-ground balance beam idea) or do twenty Jumping Jacks. The same checkpoints and many clues can be used for all the teams, with the order shuffled to avoid teams bumping into each other too many times, and possibly giving away secrets yet to be discovered.

Have the hunt end in the same location for everyone with a "treasure chest" for each team, filled with pennies they can cash in at the house for dollar store loot. Alternatively, fill the chest with gold foil-covered chocolate doubloons, candies, gum and dollar store loot the children can share between team members. Treasure chests can be small, plain boxes, spray painted with each team's name on them, or any suitable container you may find at the dollar store.

Prepare for your pirate gangs

Buy dollar store bandannas in the same colour for each team, and dream up corresponding team names. Your mini marauders could be The Blue Beard Bunch, The Black Heart Buccaneers, The Blood Red Band, and The Yellow Belly Boys.

Enlist help

This theme requires your own band of faithful adult swashbucklers to help out in a number of ways: you will need one adult Pirate Captain to accompany each group, reading the questions and controlling the pace, plus additional adults at each checkpoint, and one at the end, guarding the loot.

PARTY TIME!

When all the guests have arrived, begin by dividing them into teams. Introduce the adult Pirate Captain of each team and have them draw names from a hat to determine which children will join which gang. Help children tie on their bandannas, affix an eye patch or two, apply serious (but temporary, of course) pirate tattoos and hit the high seas.

PHOTO OP
Have teams pose with the birthday child, and make copies of the best print for each child on the team.

If your hunt ends in a park, let the kids have some playtime there—if it ends in your backyard, organize team games like Tug of War or relay races.

Follow the rest of your schedule, and enjoy the hunt.

Chapter 10

BEACH BASH

Surf's up and the kids are ready to rock!
There's always something happening
at the beach, and this party's full of ideas
that will make it seem like summer.

PLAN YOUR SCHEDULE

Activities	60 minutes
Games	15 minutes
Lunch and cake	30 minutes
Gifts	15 minutes
TOTAL	**2 HOURS**

Parties for Ages 4-6

GETTING READY

LOOT BAGS Fill colourful sand pails with beach loot like leis, picture frames, shells, sunglasses, inflatable beach balls, fish soaps and shower puffs and/or fish-shaped crackers.

Invitations

Have everyone come in beach attire—even on the coldest winter day, kids will love wearing shorts and tank tops to the party under their snowsuits, of course.

Get your decorations

Call or visit local travel agencies and beg some posters of sunny destinations to decorate the party room. Buy some brown and green Bristol board and cut out a large palm tree to stick on the wall. Get the birthday boy or girl to help you make a large sign for the front door that says something like "Welcome to Megan's Beach Club" and decorate it with a bright yellow sun and lots of colourful fish, lobsters, crabs and other underwater characters.

Plan the activities

Have several "stations" set up for various activities to keep kids busy at the beach. Buy a box of bright and colourful beads in a variety of shapes and sizes, and have one station set up where kids can make necklaces or ankle bracelets.

Have another set up where they can get a braid or two with beads and foil tips put into their hair by an expert "island" hairdresser.

Parties for Ages 4-6

Have a station just for decorative decal tattoos, and let the kids pick which one they want... and where they want it!

Have another where they can glue together wooden sticks into simple picture frames, and decorate them with small shells, glitter and stickers.

Enlist help

In order to keep the activities moving, and to ensure that each child gets a chance to do each one, try to have each station manned by one adult. Make sure your hairdresser is adept at braiding, as there will probably be a variety of hair lengths and thickness to contend with.

PARTY TIME!

Welcome guests with dollar store leis in bright colours.

Divide children into as many groups as there are activity stations, and let them get started immediately. Keep an eye on each group's progress, and switch groups as they finish each station's activity.

Play beach tunes throughout, so that the party mood stays high in between stations! Set up a mop or broom handle game of Limbo, and get the adults at the party to participate as well! Play Big Foot using loud Hawaiian shirts, Bermuda shorts, sunglasses, baseball caps and giant flip-flops.

Dress your table up with colourful picnic wares and scatter shells in the centre of the table. Serve fruit punch in plastic wineglasses with umbrellas, skewered with pineapple or orange chunks and maraschino cherries.

PHOTO OP Have the party guests takes turns standing with the birthday boy or girl under the palm tree, wearing their colourful leis. If you can develop these shots before the end of the party, trim them and fit them into the frames so the children can take them home.

IT'S A BEACH PARTY!

C h a p t e r   1 1

GARDEN TEA PARTY

A real grown-up tea party for kids (and parents too!) A charming garden tea prepared by the children is the perfect springtime backyard party.

PLAN YOUR SCHEDULE

Potting plants/ painting pots	30 minutes
Hat craft/placecards	15 minutes
Food prep	30 minutes
Changing into fancy dress	15 minutes
Tea and cake	30 minutes
Gifts	15 minutes
TOTAL	2 1/4 HOURS

Parties for Ages 4-6

This is a craft-intensive party that will move along better with a few extra pairs of adult hands to help with glueing and cutting.

LOOT BAGS Pack plastic buckets with plastic garden tools, packets of flower seeds, floral and butterfly stickers, floral notebooks, and floral hair accessories.

GETTING READY

Invitations

Ask children to come in play clothes and to bring a fancy outfit to change into. Also, ask each parent to come back a half-hour before the end of the party for "tea."

Shop for craft supplies

Purchase inexpensive clay pots at a garden store, with a rim wide enough to paint. Also purchase one potted geranium per child, and potting soil, as they will be planting blooms in their individual pots.

At the dollar store, look for inexpensive straw hats, ribbon and sprigs of fake flowers. If sewing is your thing, buy ends of floral fabric and sew long bands of fabric to decorate the hats. Alternatively, use pinking shears to cut the bands, and leave them unhemmed with a zig zag finish.

Also, look for blank placecards, or buy Bristol board or construction paper to make your own. Pick up pretty butterfly and floral stickers to decorate the placecards.

Parties for Ages 4-6

Decide on the menu

Since the plan is to have the kids "help" prepare the tea, decide on simple foods that children and adults will both enjoy. Peanut-butter sandwiches (check for allergies), egg and/or

tuna salad in mini pitas, cheese and crackers, lemonade and iced tea, and frosted cup-cakes for dessert are just suggestions—you can decide what would best suit the crowd. Don't forget to include some of the birthday child's favourites as well.

Have a contingency plan in case of rain

In a perfect world, you would be awakened the morning of the party by the sun streaming in your windows. Borrowed card tables and patio tables would be set up

around the yard, initially serving as craft tables, and then magically transforming into elegant dining tables with the addition of a few pretty cloths or even sheets.

If the weather is uncooperative, however, you may need to set up inside—crafts can be done on the kitchen floor or in a basement, and tea served wherever the guests are seated.

PARTY TIME!

Put the children to work immediately when they arrive. Have a selection of bright, quick-dry, washable paints on hand, and ask them to decorate the rims only of the clay pots. Remove the pots from the table, and let dry.

Crafts

Next, move on to the hat craft. Give the children one straw hat each, and let them select a pre-cut floral hatband or ribbon to tie around the base of the hat. Give them their choice of flowers to attach with a glue gun (under adult supervision) or white craft glue. Remove the hats from the table, and let the glue dry. If there are any boys in attendance, they may prefer to fashion a plain band of fabric into a bow tie, and decorate it with sequins, or make the hat for their mothers.

Bring on the pre-cut placecards and give each child two. Using brightly coloured markers, they can write their own names on one and their parent's name on the other, and then decorate with stickers.

Food Preparation

Move on to the kitchen, where all those little helping hands can get busy preparing the tea. Divide them into small groups where they can make sandwiches, stuff mini-pitas, stick cocktail picks into cheese cubes and arrange with crackers on small platters, and mix lemonade.

Give each child two cupcakes to frost, and offer different tinted frostings for them to choose from. Be sure to label paper plates with each child's name, so the children can proudly serve their parents a cupcake they made—and eat the other one themselves. Have extras frosted in advance for seconds.

Planting

Back to the craft table now, where an adult helper has brought

back the clay pots, and added a bucket or large container of potting soil at each table, and the geraniums. Have adults show children how to scoop soil into the bottom of the pot, pour in a little water, set in the geranium, and fill with soil. Caution the children to grasp the pots below the rim in case the paint has not set completely.

PHOTO OP
Make sure you get a photo of all the children holding their cakes, surrounding the birthday child.

Tea Party

After the children have washed up, they're ready to change into their tea party clothes. Help them keep their play clothes together by giving them each a shopping bag with their name on it. While the children are changing, an adult helper can wipe down the tables, and lay the cloths and placecards. When the children return, have them place their potted plants at their parent's places, and let them don their beautiful hats.

When the parents arrive, have the children seat them at their places. Give each child a small plate of sandwiches or cheese and crackers to serve around. Don't forget to bring out your portable stereo with a classical music CD to set the mood.

When tea is over, have children clear their own place and their parent's, and give them their plates with their cupcakes. Gather around the birthday child and sing "Happy Birthday" before serving the cake.

Follow the rest of your schedule and enjoy the party!

Chapter 12

FASHION SHOW EXTRAVAGANZA

There may be scouts from Paris and Milan begging for an invitation to this local showcase of up-and-comers! Obviously a great idea for girls, but a mixed party is not out of the question. Kids put on a fashion show and model the latest trends for their friends.

PLAN YOUR SCHEDULE

Fashion show prep	45 minutes
Actual fashion show	30 minutes
Games	30 minutes
Lunch and Cake	30 minutes
Gifts	15 minutes
TOTAL	2 1/2 HOURS

GETTING READY

Invitations

Invite the party guests to arrive in (or bring) their own outfits for a fashion show. This will give them plenty of time to decide in advance what they want to wear.

LOOT BAGS Fill make-up bags or plastic vanity containers with inexpensive makeup, fake nails, hairclips, ponytail holders, teen magazines (where age-appropriate), and each guest's cue card.

Build a runway

Relax, it's not as hard as it sounds. Concentrate on a simple T-shape runway, built from wood or mark off your floor with brightly coloured tape. Hang two curtains (or sheets) from the ceiling at the bottom of the T, where the models will enter and exit. Alternatively, you may prefer to hang a thick curtain of crepe streamers at the entrance point. Buy (or borrow) a spotlight or a strobe light (which will come in handy for years).

Organize your supplies

You're going to need sparkly nail polish, hairspray, bobby pins, clips and inexpensive make-up. If you want, you can add some dollar store feather boas, clip-on earrings and necklaces, tattoos, and hair mascara or spray colour. Get out some of your own high-heeled shoes, although the guests may feel more comfortable in their own footwear.

Decorations

Get your birthday girl to cut pictures out of fashion magazines and have her glue them onto Bristol board. Hang them around the runway area. If you're feeling particularly energetic, string some white Christmas lights along the runway.

PARTY TIME!

When all the guests arrive, divide them into two groups. One group will go into Fashion Prep, while the other group works on the cue cards.

The Fashion Prep group can be further divided into three groups, one each for nail polish, hair and makeup, rotating until all the guests are finished. Bear in mind that some girls may be uncomfortable with "the works," and may not choose to be completely made up.

The group working on their cue cards can make up fictitious "model" names, and describe their outfits in detail.* When each group is finished, switch.

Throw all the aliases into a hat, and pick them out to determine the order in which the children will be modelling. The birthday girl may choose to come out first or last, or simply to have her name thrown into the hat as well.

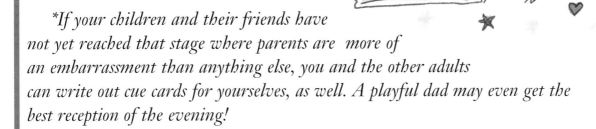

*If your children and their friends have not yet reached that stage where parents are more of an embarrassment than anything else, you and the other adults can write out cue cards for yourselves, as well. A playful dad may even get the best reception of the evening!

Have a dress rehearsal. Boys at the party may choose to take a run down the catwalk themselves, introduce the models, read the cue cards, act as official Fashion Photographer, or may simply prefer to be a part of the audience.

Set up chairs for the adults who will be attending. This is an excellent opportunity for a fashion video that can be lent out in turn to guests after the party, so they can share the fun with their families at home. Dim the lights, get some dance music on the CD player and let the show begin.

Follow the rest of your schedule and enjoy the show!

> **PHOTO OP**
> *Don't miss your chance to snap each guest sashaying her way down the runway, or have a group shot with the birthday girl in front, surrounded by the models all clapping.*

Chapter 13

LET THE GAMES BEGIN

Kids compete in a fun environment where everyone ends up a winner! This party is perfect for a sunny day, but can be moved inside if you have the space.

PLAN YOUR SCHEDULE

Team assignments /Flag prep	20 minutes
Opening ceremonies	10 minutes
Events	60 minutes
Lunch and cake	30 minutes
Closing ceremonies	15 minutes
Gifts	15 minutes
TOTAL	2 1/2 HOURS

Parties for Ages 7-10

LOOT BAGS Include whistles, chocolate medals, stop-watches, flags, water bottles and sports drinks.

Lots of helping hands are required to run this multi-event mini-event!

GETTING READY

Decide which events you will be featuring

Some easy events you may wish to consider could be: Long Jump, Tug of War, 50-yard Dash and Relay Races. Also consider some pseudo-events like Dart Throwing, Bean Bag or Ring Toss, Basketball Free Throws or Mini Putt.

Decide which countries you will be representing

Select countries with flags that are easy to draw and colour, and start the party off with team members preparing their flags. Use an encyclopedia or borrow a book from the library to get some ideas.

Get your props and supplies together

Make sure you have a stopwatch, measuring tape, a length of thick rope and a bean bag game. To confirm your official status as Olympic headquarters, have the birthday boy or girl help you make a special sign for the front door with the Olympic rings, your city and the year. Using another large piece of Bristol board, make a scoreboard with the countries listed down the left side and the events across the top. Make several mini signs for each event.

78

USE CHOCOLATE COINS!

SILVER

Have lots of markers and crayons on hand and more Bristol board to draw flags, plus broom handles or hockey sticks to mount them on.

Decide on teams in advance

With input from the birthday child, take some time dividing up the talent amongst the various teams to ensure each team has a good chance of capturing at least one medal. Aim for four-member teams, but if you have uneven numbers, let team members take turns doing double duty for each event.

TICK TICK TICK

Design and make your medals

Keep it simple because you will need one for each party guest. Spray paint sturdy cardboard circles or drink coasters, and affix them with thick lengths of dollar store ribbon in red, blue and white.

Enlist help

You will need helpers to emcee the ceremonies, paint faces, run the events, tabulate and post results. In short, you will need your very own Olympic committee.

PARTY TIME!

When all of the guests have arrived, make a big production of announcing the countries and calling each athlete up one by one. Give each team a picture of their flag and a piece of Bristol board to make their team flags. You can also buy a box of large adhesive labels at any office supply store, and let individuals draw their own flags to wear on their clothes. Or, have an adult paint the flag colours warrior-style on each athlete's face.

Have a podium area cordoned off with a colourful mini-flag garland and move your Olympic sign from the front door to this area. Have the birthday boy or girl run in first to light the Olympic torch (a tall gold candle from the dollar store is perfect), and then get each team to march in, following their flag with a team cheer of their choice. Play upbeat music to get the athletes pumped, and encourage some "muscle flexing" and good-natured camaraderie. Read out the list of events and let the games begin.

Relay races can be interspersed with other non-race events, since they are likely to be the most exciting with all the teams competing at once.

Be sure to post results on the scoreboards, as they become

PHOTO OP
Get shots of teams at the Closing ceremonies with their medals and flags.

available. For the non-team events, you can either use team averages or take the individual best scores as team winners. You might want to decide this while the party is in progress as it may be the only time you'll get to "influence" the medal chances of a team that may not be doing as well.

At the Closing Ceremonies, call out the events and winners one by one. Tabulate the grand medal winners by assigning points to events won (gold=3, silver=2, bronze=1) and call each team to the podium for the medal presentations. If you have more than three teams, call the remaining teams up to receive their participation medals, or call a tie on one of the medals.

Follow the rest of the schedule, and enjoy the games!

★THE★ SCORE

	ROUND ①	ROUND ②	FINAL
• CANADA	72	84	
• USA	66		
• BRITAIN	59		
• SPAIN			
• VENE			

C h a p t e r   1 4

MOVIE MADNESS

Budding actors and actresses will always enjoy a taste of the spotlight.

PLAN YOUR SCHEDULE

Movie Prep	30-45 minutes
Movie Shoot	30 minutes
Lunch and cake	30 minutes
Screenings	30 minutes
Gifts	15 minutes
Oscar presentations	15 minutes
TOTAL	2 1/2 HOURS

Parties for Ages 7-10

LOOT BAGS Include bullhorns, berets, autograph books, sunglasses, clipboards, teen magazines (where appropriate), extra movie posters, movie passes or video rental coupons.

Children will write, direct and star in their own movie productions. Some technical expertise will be required to run the video cameras and then hook up the cameras for viewing. This party is better suited to older children.

THIS COUPON IS GOOD FOR ONE (1) ♥ VIDEO ♥ (FROM MY COLLECTION!)

GETTING READY

Decide in advance how many groups you can manage

Each group of children will be shooting a movie, so try to keep your party limited to four groups of three to five children each.

A big consideration will also be how many video cameras you can come up with since each group will require its own.

Enlist help

Ideally, try to engage the people who lent you the video cameras—they'll know how they work. These people will also serve as informal directors, offering the children guidance and ensuring some sort of finished product will emerge at the end.

Assemble Props

Throw a variety of props into a box for each group that MUST be used in their movie.

Be Creative

Throw in a pair of winter boots, a stuffed animal, a framed photo, two rolls of toilet paper, a top hat, a pair of glasses with a fake nose and moustache, a harmonica, an overcoat, a toy stethoscope—the possibilities are endless. Look around your house and gather up the mundane, the crazy, the unusual and the everyday.

Get your supplies

Get each group a clipboard with ample lined paper for the scripts, and attach a pen on a string.

Buy tacky dollar store ceramic figurines to serve as "Oscars" for each child, or alternatively, design Oscar certificates in advance, to be handed out after the screenings.

Ensure that all the cameras are charged

Remind the owners the night before to recharge their batteries, so all cameras will be in good working order on party day.

Organize groups in advance

Taking into account the various personalities, carefully group the children who will work well together. Get input from the birthday boy or girl.

Plan your decorations

Get the birthday girl or boy to help design a "Hooray for Hollywood" sign for your front door. Cut out pictures of the latest heartthrobs from teen magazines, and paste onto Bristol board to hang in the party area.

Call your local movie theatre or video store and ask for movie posters to hang as well. Cut out stars in various sizes to put up on the walls and hang from the ceiling in the screening room. Colour photocopy your child's class photo and cut out the heads—stick these onto the smaller stars with each kid's name written in glitter glue. If you have non-classmates attending, try to get a photo ahead of time, or ask them to bring one on the day of the party.

PARTY TIME!

Divide the guests up into their respective groups and give them their prop boxes and script clipboards.

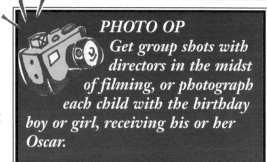

Explain that the goal is for each team to shoot a movie that will be screened after lunch. Give each group some ideas to get the ball rolling (a neighbourhood documentary, a musical, a comedy or a whodunit, for example). Encourage them to let their imaginations run wild with the only restrictions being length (no more than 10 minutes apiece, although some flexibility will be required) and that every prop must be used.

During lunch, have technical whiz friends prepare tapes for viewing. Formally invite the party guests to the screenings of the finalists in this year's Anytown Film Festival. Serve popcorn at the screenings.

While gifts are being opened, complete the Oscar certificates or list of winners.

Be Creative

While you can award for Best Actress/Actor/Screenplay/Original song, etc… add your own wacky list such as Best Drama Queen, Corniest Line, Best Joke, Best Ad Lib or Scariest Performance!

C h a p t e r   1 5

CAMP CRAZY!

Who says you've got to go to a campsite to pitch a tent?

PLAN YOUR SCHEDULE

Make trail mix	15 minutes
Hike	45 minutes
Pitch tents	30 minutes
Cook (and eat!) lunch	30 minutes
Ghost stories or games	15 minutes
Cake and gifts	15 minutes
TOTAL	**2 1/2 HOURS**

GETTING READY

Invitations

Ask guests to bring a small backpack with them for the hike.

Assemble your props

If your family already enjoys the great outdoors, you may own all the necessary equipment for a camp party. If not, get ready to make some calls because you're going to need to borrow a compass, metal BBQ skewers, two tents and a camp stove for the day… or night!

LOOT BAGS Wrap mini-flashlights, teddy bear cookies, water bottles and gummy worms in brightly coloured bandannas.

Decide what time of day the party will be

While a day party offers the same adventures as one in the evening, some activities (such as recounting ghost stories) are much more fun at night. A night camp party could even end up in a sleepover party, with fewer guests of course, but be forewarned: you are definitely sleeping outside with the Crazy Campers, and you may be awakened in the middle of the night to move the party inside.

Fun Parties For Fun Kids

Parties for Ages 7-10

Plan your hike

Draw a map of the neigh-
bourhood, or plan to hike
through nearby woods.
Prepare the route by leaving telltale signs that indicate directions—tie bright ribbons
or bandannas around trees, affix crude wooden arrows along the way, or use sidewalk
chalk clues, for example. Have the hike end up back at your house.

If you live in a quiet neighbourhood and you have parental consent, ask kids to
bring their bikes, and arrange a bike hike for older campers.

Make a sign for the door

Using a piece of Bristol board, have the birthday boy or girl design a sign for the
front door that says "Welcome to Camp Crazy—Yell if you see a bear!" or something
similarly camp-ish. Decorate your sign with twigs,
leaves, fishing lures and feathers, or draw/cut
and paste pictures of bears, deer and
snakes. Make a second sign
out of wood, and nail it to an
old hockey stick or a wooden
stake, and drive it into the
ground at your "campsite."

Shop for special camp foods

Buy lot of different ingredients
for trail mix that the children can
mix to take on their hike. Visit your
bulk retailer and buy generous quantities of raisins, peanuts, sesame sticks,

pumpkin seeds, corn nuts, shelled sunflower seeds, candy-coated chocolate candies, fish crackers and anything else you think the kids would enjoy.

Buy wieners for roasting, and of course, graham crackers, marshmallows and bars of plain chocolate to make camp favourite, S'mores.

Enlist help

Invite another adult or two to join you in the camp fun by accompanying the kids on the hike and helping to pitch the tent(s).

Party Time!

When all the guests have arrived, invite them into the kitchen to make their trail mix. Have individual bowls set out with all the ingredients and give each guest a plastic sandwich bag. Let campers assemble their trail mix with all the yummy ingredients they like.

PHOTO OP
Take a group shot at ghost story time, or individual shots of each camper with the birthday child, pointing at the wooden sign with the tent in the background.

Have each child pack a juice box and their trail mix in their backpacks, unroll your map and get hiking! Take a pair of binoculars, and let each child have a turn looking through them while you walk. Get the children involved in lookout games like spotting squirrels or birds, and sing camp songs as you go.

When you return home, let the kids pitch the tent(s), with your help, of course. If you have two tents, divide up into two groups, and have a race to see who can pitch their tent the fastest. Have a kids' plastic pool at the "campsite," and throw in a few plastic fish from the dollar store. Have a small net on hand for the kids to catch the fish, and let them have fun splashing in and out of the pool.

Help children skewer hot

dogs and watch carefully as they cook them over the camp stove. If you want to speed up the cooking process, precook the wieners slightly in the microwave before the guests arrive, so the campers are really warming them and browning the outsides, rather than cooking them.

Let campers roast marshmallows for S'mores, and have the kids assemble them by laying a piece of chocolate on a graham cracker, and topping it with a hot marshmallow and another cracker.

Gather children in a circle to tell ghost stories. If you don't know any, call a local Guide or Scout leader, or look some up at your local library. Don't be surprised if your campers are more than capable of spinning a yarn or two themselves! If the party is at night, get storytellers to shine a flashlight under their chins while recounting their spooky tales for added effect.

Follow the rest of your schedule, and enjoy the day or night!

Chapter 16

FITNESS FUN

Have some fun burning off that excess energy to the kids' favourite tunes.
This party can be adapted for other types of fitness such as Karate
or Kick-boxing, for example.

PLAN YOUR SCHEDULE

Fitness Class	30 minutes
Refreshments	10 minutes
Game show	20 minutes
Lunch and cake	30 minutes
Games	15 minutes
Gifts	15 minutes
TOTAL	2 HOURS

LOOT BAGS Place miniature shampoos, soaps and other toiletries, shower puffs, socks, headbands and water bottles in clear plastic bag. Wrap the bag in a small sports towel, and tie up with a skipping rope.

A fitness party will probably involve hiring a professional instructor or acquiring enough expertise and confidence to run a class yourself.

GETTING READY

Decide on what kind of class your child wants to do

Hire an aerobics instructor to do a class at your house. You might be able to negotiate a cut rate if you offer to include class info in the loot bags for kids who may wish to pursue the activity further following the party. Since most classes are usually an hour long, ask for a break for a half-hour of instruction.

Alternatively, you may know someone who teaches aerobics and can either come over for the party, or help YOU put together a half-hour class yourself.

Select the music

Make a list of the newest pop songs the kids all like, and record them with dance music on a tape. Don't worry about a professional mix unless your instructor has one—the kids won't care if there are gaps in the music, as long as they can recognize the tunes.

Decide on the number of children you can invite

This will depend on how large your space is, and how many children can be safely accommodated. Do not crowd participants—they should have at least an arm's length on either side of them, as well as front and back.

Parties for Ages 7-10

Decorations

Get the birthday boy or girl to help you paste pictures from fitness magazines onto Bristol board to decorate your gym area. Hang up skipping ropes, sports posters, boxing gloves, nets filled with balls, running shoes and any other fitness/sporting paraphernalia you have hanging around your house or garage.

Organize a "quiz show" type game

Using an encyclopedia, library books, kids' trivia cards, sports magazines and the daily newspaper, come up with 10-15 sports, health and fitness questions for each group. Use categories where questions become more challenging as you go along and have teams "buzz in" with the correct answers. Alternatively, just go from team to team, asking each a question and scoring accordingly.

Be Creative

Ask simple questions such as "What colour is (your home hockey team's) jersey?" or "Name three professional football teams," or "Name the four food groups," or "How many miles are there in a marathon?" Throw in a few challenging questions that could decrease in point value each time you provide a hint or clue.

Organize the groups in advance

With input from the birthday child, divide up the talent between the teams. Pick only one winning team and present them with some crazy trophy from the dollar store and call it the 1st Annual Fitness Cup.

Make up some funny Fitness Certificates to be handed out at the end of the party. Try something semi-official like this: "This is to certify that Christine H. sweated and panted through 30 minutes of intense aerobic activity to earn this Certificate of Fitness, at Jessica M's Birthday Party, June 2/??"

PARTY TIME!

When all the guests have arrived, introduce the instructor and have him/her show a few moves in advance. Bearing in mind that this might be the first time some of the children have participated in this type of organized fitness class, let them practise a bit before starting the music so they feel more comfortable.

PHOTO OP
Take individual shots of the kids with the birthday boy or girl and the fitness instructor, or take action shots of each during the fitness class.

Immediately following the class, serve platters of fresh fruit and bottled water, or small cups of sports drinks. Let the kids chat and relax for a few minutes before starting the sports quiz show.

Divide into teams and give each team captain a party horn, kazoo or bicycle horn to use to "ring in" the correct answer. If using party horns, get the ones that make noise and unfurl when you blow into them—they add to the excitement during the game. Explain the rules and how the scoring will work.

After lunch, organize a few fun games, keeping the fitness theme in mind— keep the same teams and run some relay races such as Bigfoot and wheelbarrow races.

Follow the rest of your schedule and enjoy the exercise!

Chapter 17

CREATE A CARNIVAL!

A backyard carnival with activities galore will keep kids entertained for the whole afternoon! A sunny day is just what you need, but moving inside if necessary is not impossible.

IT'S CARNIVAL! COME PARTY!! RAIN OR SHINE!!

tape

cardboard sun!

PLAN YOUR SCHEDULE

Carnival games and lunch	90 minutes
Cake & gifts	30 minutes
TOTAL	2 HOURS

Parties for Ages 7-10

LOOT BAGS

In addition to the party loot they've already collected in their prize bags, throw in a clown nose, face paint, stickers, cotton candy and small bags of peanuts in the shell.

Lots of pre-party organization, lots of set-up, lots of adult help… but lots of fun!

GETTING READY

Decide on what "booths" you're going to have

Include face painting, a photo booth, ring or beanbag toss, Bingo and a tattoo booth for sure. In addition to the above, try any (or all!) of the following suggestions:

Guess How Many

Have a jar full of gumballs (or any other candy) and let guests guess how many there are—closest without going over takes the jar home. Alternatively, have a Guess How Old My Dad Is booth, or better yet, ask a good-natured grandparent to sit at the booth. (If they can't make it, use an 8x10 photo instead.) Award a prize to the closest guesser.

Jellybean Jumble

Buy gourmet jellybeans in as many flavours as you can, and have blindfolded guests guess what kind they're eating. (Pour all the jellybeans into a large bowl, blindfold guests one at a time, let them blindly select five jellybeans from the bowl, check which ones they've picked, and let them start eating.)

Sucker Pull

Buy a bag of suckers and blacken the ends of a few of the sticks. Stick them into a block of spray-painted or decorated Styrofoam, concealing the blackened ends. Let guests pull one sucker each—those who pull one with a blackened end win a prize—others at least get to keep their suckers!

"Beat the Pro" Mini Golf

Set up a single mini-golf hole, using obstacles like decorated shoeboxes or containers, or create a hump by placing a rolled-up newspaper under the surface of your putting green. Have the "pro" putt first against each child, and award a prize to anyone who ties or scores lower than the "pro."

Fortune Teller

Have a fortune teller at the party, dressed in a brightly coloured skirt, with lots of beads, hoop earrings, oversized rings and a scarf on her head. Your fortune teller can dispense funny generic fortunes or, alternatively, ask parents secretly before the party for some personal tidbits about their child that will leave the kids marvelling at the fortune teller's skills. For example: find out how many brothers and sisters the child has, pet names, best friends, trips they've been on recently or are about to take, a favourite sport, movie star or musical group, and go from there.

Parties for Ages 7-10

Shell Game

Get three identical containers and place a small ball or checker piece under one. Move them around quickly on a flat surface and have one guest at a time try to guess which one it's under. Award a prize for each correct guess. Have your shell game "carney" practise his or her sleight-of-hand beforehand, and see if s/he can stump the guests.

Assemble Props

Based on the booths you and your child have selected, ensure you have all the appropriate items for each.

Some booths may require a small table, such as the Shell Game and the Jelly Bean Jumble, but others can be improvised.

A makeshift tent would be fun for the fortune teller, a stool can be set up for the Sucker Pull, and the Guess How Many booth too—with a box below to collect written guesses.

On the morning of the party, decide if you'll be indoors or outside, and set up the booths.

Make tickets

Have the birthday child help design a sheet of tickets, and photocopy onto coloured paper. Although tickets aren't necessary, they add to the fun of visiting the carnival.

suggestion: USE an old dust-sheet to protect your carpet!

non-toxic face-paint!

GLITTER LOTS!

Get your decorations

Buy LOTS of colourful balloons to decorate your party area.

Fun Parties For Fun Kids

Parties for Ages 7-10

If you buy helium balloons, guests can take one home with them, but if they're too costly, just tie big bunches of dollar store specials all over.

Have the birthday boy or girl make a colourful Bristol board sign for each booth, and decorate with glitter glue and metallic confetti. Be sure to indicate how many tickets each activity costs.

Affix the signs to wooden stakes and stick them in the ground outside in front of each booth, or tape them up in your party area inside.

Shop for Prizes

Go crazy in the dollar store! Look for packages of multiple prizes like rings, balls, pencils, bubble gum, plastic games, sunglasses, kaleidoscopes and stickers, and load your basket up. Prizes don't have to be expensive, but you will need a bunch, so visit a few stores in your area for variety. Label lunch bags or inexpensive gift bags for each child to collect their prizes as they play the carnival games.

Enlist help

If you've gotten this far, you've probably realized that this is not a party you should attempt on your own. The number of helpers you're going to need will, of course, depend on the number of booths you're going to run. You won't need one person for each booth, since most adults can do double or even triple duty if called upon, but don't scrimp either. Hire a friendly teenager or two to pitch in for a couple of hours—if you're lucky, or just very persuasive by nature, someone might just consent to dress as a clown!

PARTY TIME!

When all the guests have arrived, give them each the denomination of tickets that would allow them to visit each booth once or twice.

Let them get their faces painted first, and then move on to the photo booth.

Let the kids wander from booth to booth at will, gathering them all together as a group midway through the party to play Bingo.

Bring out small bags of popcorn and cotton candy at intervals, and even caramel apples if you feel like making them the night before. Serve hot dogs before or during Bingo, with small bags of French fries or potato chips.

Set the mood with calliope music, or have the kids' favourite tunes playing on the portable stereo.

Follow the rest of your schedule and enjoy the carnival!

PHOTO OP
Have each child pose at the photo booth with the guest of honour...after their faces have been painted, of course.

Chapter 18

FOOTBALL FEVER

Welcome to training camp where everyone makes the cut!
A fall day would be perfect for a game of touch football—provided the kids
all survive training camp, of course.

PLAN YOUR SCHEDULE

Training Camp	45 minutes
Touch football game	30 minutes
Lunch and cake	30 minutes
Gifts	15 minutes
TOTAL	2 HOURS

Parties for Ages 7-10

LOOT BAGS Include trading cards, whistles, sports drinks, adhesive bandages, stopwatches, bullhorns, water bottles, kids' sports magazines and small logo items.

GETTING READY
Decide on where you're going to hold training camp

A park or school field are your best bets, particularly if they're within walking distance, or you can have it in your backyard if you have a lot of space.

Design an obstacle course

Obstacle courses can be as long or as short as you want them to be, and they're very easy to design. Elements can be broken up with running segments to lengthen the course, and distractions along the way will add to the fun.

A sample course could be something like this:

Run 25 yards – Run 8-12 car tires, knees-up style – Catch a football, while being squirted with water – Run a zigzag pattern around the pylons – Throw the football through a swinging tire – Catch another football while being squirted with water – Run 25 more yards, jumping 4 hurdles along the way – Spike the football in the end zone.

Get your props together

Call your local garage, gas station, auto wrecking yard, etc… and beg old tires for the party that you can return the following day.

Have at least 4-6 footballs on hand to keep the

Fun Parties For Fun Kids

Parties for Ages 7-10

guests moving through the obstacle course. Call your city or town's recreation department, your kids' school, or anyone you might know to borrow pylons, or make them yourself, with cardboard boxes and bright fluorescent tape or paint.

Buy water pistols to squirt at the kids during the obstacle course, or use an oversized water gun for more wet fun.

Decide on teams in advance for touch football

Divide up the talent with the help of the birthday boy or girl, and give each team a solid football name like the Panthers or the Dolphins. Buy bandannas in two colours that the players can wear during the game to differentiate the teams.

Decorations

Put up football posters, hang helmets, pennants and cleats. Have the birthday boy or girl cut out pictures from sports magazines and the newspaper, and paste them onto Bristol board. Make a Bristol board sign for the front door that reads "Tyler's Training Camp—Only the Strong Survive" or some other hyped-up greeting to welcome guests.

Enlist help

Get a dad or two to help run the drills during Training Camp, timing the Obstacle Course, throwing the football and squirting the participants. Buy each dad a whistle to wear around his neck, and a baseball cap with a sticker that says Coach, and encourage the dads to assume the persona on and off the field during the party.

PARTY TIME!

Once all the players have arrived, start with a team meeting, where the "Head Coach" rallies the troops for Training Camp and the big game.

Take the kids out to the field where the other coaches are waiting for the players (actually guarding the Obstacle Course which was assembled an hour earlier). Introduce the coaches by their sporty nicknames and divide up the teams.

PHOTO OP
Take team photos with coaches where everyone strikes a menacing pose, or get individual shots of players as they come through the Obstacle Course.

Coaches could start by running some military-style drills—Jumping Jacks, push-ups, running a lap or two, for example.

Coaches can then demonstrate the obstacle course, and draw names to determine the order in which the guests will go through.

Use a stopwatch to time each player's foray through the obstacle course, and keep track of the best time throughout as the "Time to Beat." If you have extra time, kids would probably love the chance to go through again, trying to beat their original times.

When training camp is over, have a game of touch football, where the coaches can call the plays and help plan strategy, or participate as player-coaches as well.

Follow the rest of the schedule and enjoy the sport!

TYLER'S TRAINING CAMP
ONLY THE STRONG SURVIVE
(BUT EVERYBODY ☆ HAS FUN!)

C h a p t e r   1 9

STOP THE PRESSES!

*Reporters-in-training will be able to show off
their very own newspapers.*

**PLAN YOUR
SCHEDULE**

Press pass craft	15 minutes
Newspaper assembly	45 minutes
Games	15 minutes
Lunch and cake	30 minutes
Gifts	15 minutes
TOTAL	2 HOURS

Parties for Ages 7-10

This idea is suitable for older children, ideally those who enjoy projects and can sit still long enough to complete them.

LOOT BAGS
Try to find the pocketbooks that show two almost identical pictures side-by-side where you have to spot the differences, also notebooks, pens, disposable cameras and/or photo albums

GETTING READY
Decide on the size of the newspaper the kids will produce

You can have a 2-page newspaper (front and back), using an 11x17 sheet of paper. Get a friend with some design knowledge (or just a good eye for design) or come up with a basic layout for both sides, and draw it in. Go over your pencil layout carefully with a thin black marker.

Some elements to include:
- a space across the top for a banner
- various size boxes for photos (hand-drawn pictures) with lined space for copy (the story)
- lined space for an editorial
- a box for a 3-day weather forecast with space for accompanying weather graphics the kids can add—rain, snow and sun, for example
- lined space for a book review plus a 5-title Bestseller List
- lined space for a CD, movie or concert review
- boxes for sports standings, fashion photos and comics
- lined space for an advice column, food column or recipe of the day

Designate whatever spaces you have left for ads.

Parties for Ages 7-10

Get copies made

Take your layout to a copy shop and make enough double-sided copies for each child to have two (and then some, to be on the safe side)—one for a rough draft and one for a good copy.

While you're there, have a colour copy made of the school class picture, and cut out heads to use as ID on the press passes. Ask non-class friends to bring along photos of themselves. If they forget, get them to draw a funny face, or cut one out of a magazine.

Assemble supplies

Make sure you have ample supplies of pencils, erasers and coloured pencils available for the number of children you're inviting. Have markers available for the press passes.

Have samples of simple items such as weather forecasts, comic strips, bestseller lists and advice columns pasted on Bristol board for kids to use as reference. Have flyers and fashion magazines available for kids who would rather cut out ads and photos than draw them.

Design the press passes

Using index cards or pre-cut pieces of stiff cardboard, get the birthday boy or girl

"Deadline"

to help you draw on each card: a box for each child's photo, and lines on which kids can print their names, the name of their newspaper, and the name of the event. Affix a long shoelace or ribbon to the press pass, so the children can wear them around their necks at the party.

Decorations

Use newsprint to cover your table, or get the birthday child to make personalized placemats out of newspaper for each guest by writing his or her name across the "mat" in bright fluorescent marker. Borrow a book from the library that shows how to fold paper hats, and make party hats out of newsprint.

Make a sign for the front door that says "Alex's Press Club—Members Only," and decorate with headlines, news stories and photos.

PARTY TIME!

Once all the guests have arrived, get them started on their press passes. Have a completed sample on hand, and encourage them to come up with newsy nicknames for themselves like "Scoop" or "Hound Dog."

PHOTO OP
Have a big enough space on the front-page layout for a group shot that can be pasted on by the end of the party.

Distribute the blank newspapers and get kids started. Have them name their newspaper and design their banner. Give them some choices of typical newspaper names like Star, Gazette, Sun, Herald, Free Press, Times, Journal, or the Post.

Have the headline story be the birthday party and make sure they cover the 5 W's: Who, What, Where, When and Why. Encourage them to interview and get quotes from other guests and the birthday boy or girl.

Since a good reporter often has to rely on his or her memory, play a game of "What's Missing" with items associated with being a reporter: a pen, a small tape recorder, a notebook, a camera, a running shoe, a photograph and a map, to name a few.

THE ★ STAR
"A NEWSPAPER FOR KIDS, BY KIDS"

You can also write the names of a few well-known personalities on scraps of paper, throw them into a hat, and have each child select one. The others then ask reporter-style questions, trying to determine that person's identity. Be sure to include the school principal and the birthday boy or girl among the pop, movie and sports celebrities, and be prepared to give generous hints if they're on the wrong track.

Follow the rest of the schedule and enjoy the news!

Chapter 20

SUPERSTAR!

Come as your favourite celebrity and get ready to show your stuff!
This is a combination celebrity party and talent show for
the entertainers in the crowd.

PLAN YOUR SCHEDULE

Talent show rehearsals	30 minutes
Talent Show	15 minutes
Games	30 minutes
Lunch and cake	30 minutes
Gifts	15 minutes
TOTAL	2 HOURS

SONG & DANCE CONTEST
JAZZ, TAP, FREESTYLE

SUPER STAR

JAZZ

GETTING READY

LOOT BAGS
Include autograph books, sunglasses, trading cards, teen magazines (where appropriate), fake nails and/or jewellery.

Invitations

Make sure the invitations specify that kids should come dressed as their favourite celebrities.

Decide on the talent show format

Grouping kids together for a talent show is a good idea since some will be too shy to perform on their own. Gather some ideas such as skits, stand-up comedy, dance numbers and singing acts for performers to consider.

Design a stage area

Hang two sheets from the ceiling, and tape off a large area for a stage. Get the birthday boy or girl to help you make a banner to hang above your stage area that reads "Talent Contest—Today 3 p.m."

Assemble your Props

Borrow a couple of the current pop CD's and movie soundtracks that are popular with kids, since most will probably want music at some point during their performances.

Consider renting a karaoke machine for the evening, or borrow one if possible. The kids can use it during the show, and will certainly enjoy it for the whole party. (Moms and dads may be surprised at how much fun it can be for them too!)

Get a strobe light or spotlights to add special effects when introducing groups.

Fun Parties For Fun Kids

Parties for Ages 7-10

Have some additional wardrobe props like feather boas, clip-on earrings, sunglasses, tiaras, gloves and hats, in case kids want to add to their costumes.

Have the birthday child cut out celebrity photos from magazines and glue them onto Bristol board. Cut out stars in various sizes and stick them on the walls.

Organize your games

Have a Celebrity Scramble by putting together a list of ten celebrities and scrambling the letters in their names. At game time, hand out a photocopy to each guest, and see who can unscramble the names in the least amount of time.

Plan a game of "Future Stars." Buy gift bags in five different colours and get paper in corresponding colours to match. Cut enough small squares for each guest to have one in each colour.

Label bags:

    (1) City

    (2) Car

    (3) Famous actor, singer or sports figure

    (4) Pet name

    (5) Any Number.*

Note: these sample categories would be suitable for girls—you can easily change the labels for a mixed party.

Parties for Ages 7-10

At game time, have each guest write an entry for each of the bags, shake them up, and have each party guest pull one square from each bag. Put the squares together and predict what the future stars' lives are going to be like—where they'll live, what kind of car they will drive, who they will marry, what they change their name to (this is the pet name) and how many children they will have.

Enlist help

A few extra hands will come in very handy to play music and work lights during the talent show, as well as helping with the games.

Fun Parties For Fun Kids

PARTY TIME!

When all the guests have arrived, group them according to how they're dressed. For example, put all your musicians together, movie stars and sports figures. Give them time (and be ready with ideas!) to get their acts together, and be available for lighting and music consultations.

PHOTO OP
Take a shot of each guest with the birthday boy or girl and use the Talent Show sign as the backdrop.

Have an adult act as a Judge for the talent show who will mark based on criteria such as Creativity, Originality and Entertainment Value. At the end of the show, call each group up individually and have the Judge read out the scores for each category, as well as the final score… which could very easily end in a multi-team tie!

In order to expedite the Future Stars game, divide guests into two groups and assign an adult to each group. Have the adult record the children's responses to each category, encouraging exotic locales, fancy cars and unusual pet names.

Let the birthday child pull his or her squares first, and tell each star-to-be what they can expect in the future: "Sara, when you grow up you're going to live in Paris (city), drive a

YAY! CLAP CLAP CLAP CLAP

limo (car), get married to Bobby Rocker (famous musician) change your name to Fifi (pet name) and have 12 (number) kids!"

Help spice up the readings with some good-natured teasing and looks of feigned shock and surprise. The combinations are sure to bring out the giggles in the crowd!

Serve fancy "hors d'oeuvre" style finger foods with cocktail toothpicks on silver platters, and fancy drinks with speared fruit in plastic wine glasses.

Follow the rest of your schedule and enjoy the stars!